D0811551

APR   2010

NOW, THAT'S BIG

SKOKIE PUBLIC LIBRARY

Published by Creative Education
P.O. Box 227, Mankato, Minnesota 56002
Creative Education is an imprint of The Creative Company
www.thecreativecompany.us

Design and Production by The Design Lab
Printed in the United States of America

Photographs by Alamy (nagelestock, Photo Network, GEORGE AND
MONSERRATE SCHWARTZ, Tom Till), Getty Images (Alfred Eisenstaedt/
Pix Inc./Time & Life Pictures, Frederic Lewis, Popperfoto), iStockphoto
(Magdalena Marczewska)

Copyright © 2009 Creative Education
International copyright reserved in all countries. No part of this book may
be reproduced in any form without written permission from the publisher.

Library of Congress Cataloging-in-Publication Data
Riggs, Kate.
Mount Rushmore / by Kate Riggs.
p. cm. — (Now that's big!)
Includes index.
ISBN 978-1-58341-705-8
1. Mount Rushmore National Memorial (S.D.)—Juvenile literature. I. Title.
F657.R8R54 2009   978.3'93—dc22   2007052341

First edition

9 8 7 6 5 4 3 2 1

RUSHMORE

BY KATE RIGGS

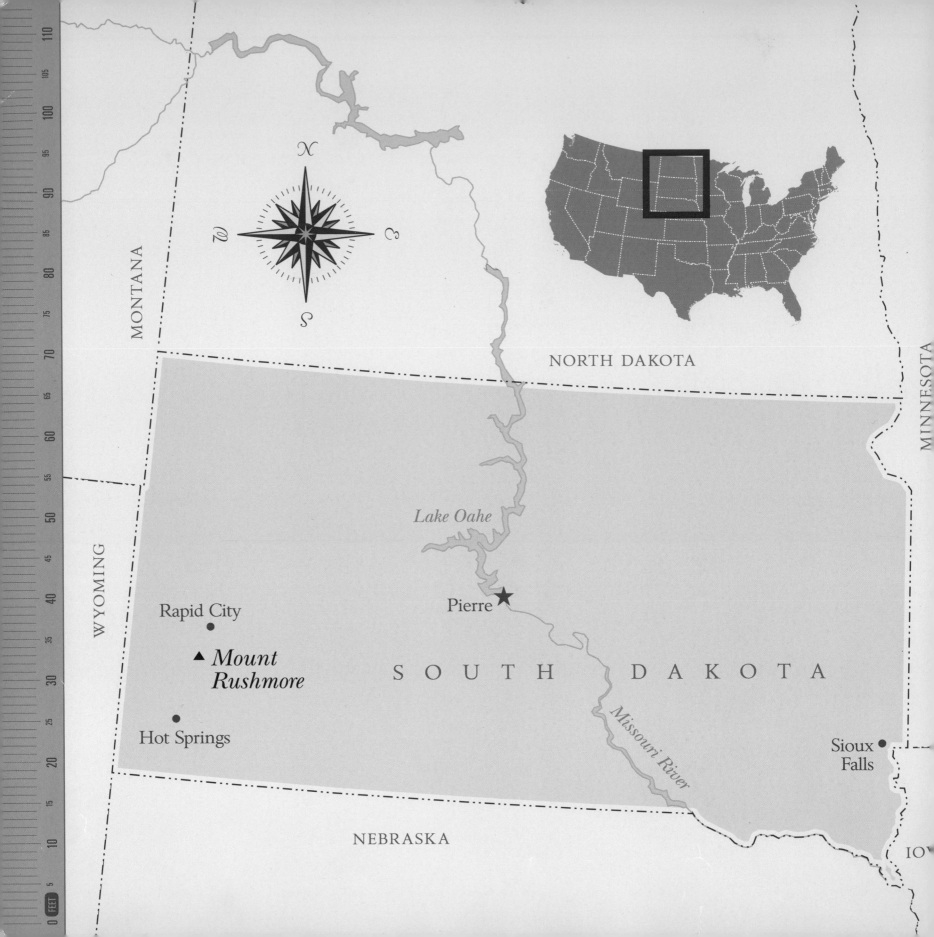

MONTANA

NORTH DAKOTA

MINNESOTA

WYOMING

Lake Oahe

Rapid City
•

▲ *Mount Rushmore*

Hot Springs
•

Pierre ★

S O U T H   D A K O T A

Missouri River

Sioux Falls
•

NEBRASKA

IOW

Mount Rushmore is a sculpture carved out of a mountain. It is in the state of South Dakota. It shows the heads of four American presidents. People in South Dakota made Mount Rushmore to get other people to visit their state.

George Washington's face was the first to be sculpted

6

A man named Gutzon (*GOOT-zahn*) Borglum came up with the plan for Mount Rushmore. He chose four presidents to be in his sculpture. Their names are George Washington, Thomas Jefferson, Theodore Roosevelt, and Abraham Lincoln.

The Needles was the first site thought of for the sculpture

8

There are lots of big, pointy pieces of granite near Mount Rushmore. They are called the Needles.

The mountain of Mount Rushmore is made out of a hard rock called granite. About 400 people worked on the mountain starting in 1927. They used dynamite to break up the rock and make shapes.

1927

People who watched Mount Rushmore being built took lots of pictures.

People started visiting Mount Rushmore before it was finished

10

Each head on Mount Rushmore is 60 feet (18 m) tall. The last head was finished in 1939. People celebrated every time a new part of the sculpture was finished.

The people who carved the faces worked at dangerous heights

Each head has a nose that is about 20 feet (6 m) long. Each mouth is 18 feet (5.5 m) wide. The noses and mouths are as big as some small boats!

Work ended in 1941 when money for the project ran out

People come from all over the United States to see Mount Rushmore. They think of the giant heads as pieces of art. The sculpture also reminds people of the good leaders the U.S. has had.

The Avenue of Flags is at the bottom of Mount Rushmore

16

People can see all 50 U.S. states' flags as they walk through the Avenue of Flags.

Today, more than two million people visit Mount Rushmore every year. People walk through the Avenue of Flags to get to the viewing **platform**. From there, they can see Mount Rushmore clearly.

Animals like prairie dogs and bison live close to Mount Rushmore.

Prairie dogs eat mostly grasses and plants that have flowers

18

People can see lots of birds and animals close to Mount Rushmore. Deer, bighorn sheep, and chipmunks live in the mountains. It is hot there in the summer when most people visit.

The Crazy Horse Memorial shows a famous Indian leader

20

The Crazy Horse Memorial is another big sculpture in South Dakota. It is close to Mount Rushmore.

Mount Rushmore is a big sculpture that means a lot to America. As long as the rock lasts, people will keep on visiting it!

Mount Rushmore is part of an area called the Black Hills in South Dakota.

GLOSSARY

celebrated—*did something fun to mark a special day*

platform—*a place where people can stand to better see something*

presidents—*people who are the leaders of their country*

sculpture—*a work carved into stone or some other hard material that shows what someone or something looked like*

READ MORE ABOUT IT

Anderson, William. *M Is for Mount Rushmore: A South Dakota Alphabet*. Chelsea, Mich.: Sleeping Bear Press, 2005.

Patrick, Jean L. S. *Who Carved the Mountain? The Story of Mount Rushmore*. Keystone, S.D.: Mount Rushmore History Association, 2005.

24